ACKNOWLEDGEMENTS

108 DAYS OF GRATITUDE

also by Tanya Gervasi
Della Bellezza E Del Silenzio
Look Again

TANYA GERVASI

ACKNOWLEDGEMENTS

108 DAYS OF GRATITUDE

MY NEW COLLECTION

Copyright © 2023 Tanya Gervasi

All rights reserved. This book or any portion thereof may not be reproduced or used in any manner whatsoever without the express written permission of the publisher except for the use of brief quotations in a book review.

ISBN: 9798388611253

Imprint: Independently published

Cover design by Alex Meyer

First self-published in England in 2023

www.inhergenius.com

Gratitude is the wine for the soul. Go on. Get Drunk.
           -   Rumi

Contents

Foreword..................................ix
Poems................................. 1
Thank you...........................85
About the author.....................87

Foreword

In 2021, I was a nanny to a family of 3 small children and my life was this: wake up at 4'30AM, make a protein smoothie, read some news, get dressed, cycle for 1 hour (over half of it uphill), start work by preparing breakfast for the kids and parents, prepare the lunchbox, get kids ready for school, get baby to nap, remake the beds and tidy the bedrooms, put wash machine on, prepare lunch for parents, clean, have lunch with parents, fold laundry, take baby on a walk, cycle back 45 minutes (thank goodness downhill mostly), take a shower, prepare food for myself and hubby, read a few pages of a book, sleep (I'd usually fall asleep at 8PM). Nothing exciting. Nothing inspiring. I felt like factory workers must feel: tired and resentful.

Routines can be a wonderful thing and help us a lot, but if they are not set by us and we must obey someone else's schedule, problems begin to arise - that is when you don't look after your own cup and make sure it's full, firstly for yourself. No matter the amount of spiritual work throughout the years I too slip into patterns where I allow my energy to be taken from me, basically I let go and think the form must change, when in reality it's the core that moulds the form.
After five months into that job I was not a nice person, I let it consume me. So I thought to challenge myself to switch my

mood and up my energy by shifting my attention: for 108 days I'd write poems giving thanks to what is.

Poems rather than mere gratitude lists allowed me to embody the poet archetype - someone who notices what the majority overlook. A poet not only notices how leaves vibrate to the touch of the wind, creating music, but also what that vibration does to his own body and spirit... how a thought can send an oscillation down our spine, to our legs and make its way to the ground.

When I allowed myself to settle into the present day, I began to notice all the things that bring me joy and laughter, lifting my spirit. The more I guided my focus toward things I loved, the lighter I became and the happier I was even waking up at 4'30AM. Waking up that early got me to bike in a desert city and by the time I'd get to the top of the hill I could bathe in the first sunrise. Now that I don't do it, I miss that feeling. I miss the feeling of relief I'd feel getting to the top of Muswell Hill with my legs shaking from fatigue. And this is the point. A lot of what we live, our current lifestyle, the current job, is 1. temporary and 2. the result of past decisions. I took back the responsibility of the fact that I chose to get that job for a year. I could've probably got a new one, but it would've yielded the same results in terms of feelings, if my attitude didn't change. So I changed my attitude, I gave thanks everyday and I decided it was enough. Don't be intimidated by the word "poetry". Poetry is a predisposition of the soul and everyone can temporarily become a poet. And should you wish to remain one for the rest of your life the world will thank you in return.

So I invite you to write your own 108 days of gratitude as you read mine. Allow yourself to be touched by those beautiful moments in time upon which life thrives.

This is my wish: when life gets overwhelming, stop, open your ears, let the birds become louder than traffic noise; when you lose yourself chasing someone else's visions, stop, look down and breathe; when you don't have time for you, stop, take a bath and give thanks.

Acknowledge your life moments, for those remain when all else changes.

Tanya Gervasi
December 2022

PS. Why 108 days? Truth be told, I find this number exuding a finite and healing energy. If you research it you will learn that a mala has 108 beads, the mantra is to be recited 108 times, in numerology 108 echoes the same frequency of infinite potential. Moreover, you might discover that the diameter of the Sun is 108 times that of the Earth. So in short it's a number deemed sacred in many Eastern traditions, and not only.

1.

sitting on my yoga mat
I noticed the goldfinch singing
I'm alive!
thank you
yet I forget to live
everyday
I feel running an imaginary hamster wheel
I am alive
I cling to that feeling
until I feel myself living
I breathe!
thank you
in and out, in and out
I am at the doorway
I see!
thank you
the blue sky above the city of London
and the seagulls which take me by the sea
with their keows, what a blessing to have these birds
cut through the city's skyline,
anyone who's ever been on a beach would know

they belong there
whereas here, they only aid our escapes
as we close our eyes and dream
of warmth and salty water
thank you

2.

sometimes I manage to be
the master of my time,
it bends to my needs
like this morning riding bikes
in the company of Love
thank you
the smell of coffee and
the sight of fresh bread and pastries
puts a smile on my face
slowing me down
thank you
my eyes blessed with the sight
of the royal family of swans
six babies I count

watching them gracefully sail
the waters of Hampstead Heath
thank you

3.

we often complain
of cleaning and tidying and decluttering, too
not realising, as we so often do,
how those botherings mean
we got a roof on our head
and too much to fit in
thank you
as friends open their doors to me
I scan through their soul
the past among stuff
the present in their eyes
the future I read in those unfinished projects,
they allow me to whirlwind
through their lives
how precious of a gift, that of trust
I bring no destruction

only peace
thank you

4.

then one day I blossomed
I thought to myself
catching my image reflected back to me in a window
there I see my grandmother nodding at me
and my mother smiling
all their stress and tears, barracking and punishments
have not been in vain
I am pieces of their best self
suddenly I realised
I am in excellent company
thank you

5.

today
what if you get that job

what if the sun's out in London
what if the people you meet are nice
what if your biggest dream comes true
what if you are safe
what if you get to eat exactly what you craved
what if you do live your fairytale
what if it works out
what if you find the cream you were looking for
what if what if what if
I couldn't contain the tears
as I breathlessly observed all those what ifs
fall into place at once
thank you
thank you
thank you
how can I ever doubt again?
or, better
how can I ever not notice again the perfection of a day?

6.

it smells of earth and worms and clay

the minute water turns into rain
I love waking up to the sound
of drops hitting the window
birds chatting
my partner typing
the smell of coffee
and me wondering whether to stay
or get up
to go - where?
can I stay between the worlds
swinging back and forth?
allow me
thank you

7.

a yin yang life
begins with a yin yang day
a bike tour followed by yoga
time alone after a morning together
visiting a nature reserve whilst in the city
thank you

the food found at every corner
a taste of any country you miss
today my man and I
can say we crossed the ocean
eating an all American dream
thank you

8.

on my balcony
there is a laurel
with a long skinny trunk
and a not-too-rich crown
among the other plants I've got
he has always looked a little off
albeit having the most exquisite bush of thyme
wrapping it like a ballet gown
out of compassion I have decided
to turn him into the king of the garden
so on one branch I hung a shiny jewel
and next to it a bright yellow feeder
I also added a bowl of water

full of gratitude he now shines
attracting all sorts of life
I wake up to goldfinch and sparrows' songs
and feel so much joy
because of the bird-watching sanctuary
created right outside my home
thank you

9.

what about a life with no responsibilities
on the horizon
the sky is clear and the ocean blue
I am soaking up the sun reading a book
thank you
even when there is no sun to soak
I love going on a walk
taking the time to breathe and observe
what is and what is not
this is the life I chose
thank you

10.

I love my job
something I used to say
without meaning it for a moment
when I was a model
today with my hands in the soil
my cheeks red from the sun
the sweat sliding down
and smelling so not ladylike
I paused happily
thinking
I love my job
thank you
my senses startled
by the smells of plants I could recognise
good memory! I tell myself
lemon grass, chamomile and thyme
rosemary, mint and lemon balm
oh the uses in the kitchen
my imagination began to stride
thank you

11.

sweet are the times
you can sit on the ground
outside a supermarket
to listen
someone playing the guitar
her voice is so divine
and those around immersed in their phantom futures
suddenly arrived in the here and now
can we have more of these artists
make music at every corner so
we'd never want to depart from ourselves
the present would be enough
thank you

12.

to get home tired
a head full of thoughts
I acknowledged my need
to lie on my mat to do some yin

only five minutes turn into sixty
I empty out
and fill my cup
thank you

13.

I knew this day would come, when
I don't have energy to write, dare I say
I did live my day in the best possible way
yet I lack words to describe it
so tonight I raise a glass
to friendships
to barbeques
to booze
to the lobster that gave me his life
to lambs and pigs and cows
to Love always by my side
and to myself still here
even in silence
thank you

14.

suddenly struck
by the realisation
that nothing disappears
not one thing we have lived leaves our body
not one person that has touched us is ever forgotten
we are fools to believe
to be able to start a new book
the book is always the same, the book of our life
yet we can start a new chapter
with new stories
thank you
I can surf a blank page
usually then, the sea is calm with no big waves
but today is the day tsunamis hit
suddenly rising from my past
begins a race toward the shore
stroll after stroll I try to ignore
the big wall advancing, ferocious
what does it want? again again again
how many more times do I need to glide away?
I'm slow today

I'm under
it's hard to breathe
don't want to hear
the sound of silence enveloping my body
I'm gone
until I see a hand
a random man dancing at the stoplight, on my way to work
I laugh and breathe
I don't manage to hold onto it
but it's clear to me now, I focus to look for another hand
so I scan reality and notice everything
it is the day that even trash on the street
becomes my shore
thank you

15.

if I had three lines to describe this day,
I'd have an unexpected brunch with Love and a friend
going plant hunting across Shoreditch and forgetting groceries on the way

then finish the day in the most perfect way, flowing on water exploring the fair
a day full of movement and food and play
thank you - for more lines

16.

when I saw the bed
I thought how great
I would most likely fall asleep
but as soon as the needle touched my wrist
I laughed at myself
how naive of me to think I could sleep through the pain
- and yet don't we? -
as a consequence my thoughts began their quest
to make a meaning
of all the pain I was feeling
I chose it consciously at least
still some say we always choose our pain,
only we forget about it the moment our soul incarnates
then why would someone choose consciously the pain
as if memory would not withhold

the spirit of the symbol unless carried on the skin
hour after hour
the philosophical questions faded
leaving space to a plastic fish
placed upside down in a hole in the wall
- how curious -
perhaps now it's a good time
to practise escapism
although it's too intense
I see some blood
- God, do I even love myself? -
after some time
I know the pain will dim
leaving space
to a beautiful raven's feather
in which I see the dance we all play
pain - space - beauty
thank you

17.

always there for me

you are

the feet onto which my wings rest

you are

the wings under which I hide my head

you are

a bright light walking next to me

you are

you offer me stability and security

a constant high level of attention

I was not used to but have learned to cherish dearly

you are

Love

in the purest form

you are

noble, a chivalry of heart I thought men long lost

you are

all elements in one, dancing through life

with me

you are

my love

thank you

18.

the late afternoon sun
was highlighting
the contour of a weeping willow
curling on the bank
at the same time the canal's water was reflecting
the white light onto the surroundings
all sparkled of life right before symbolic death
I was in a rush
yet one glimpse over the scenery
slingshot me in a painting
I have in my head from childhood
I am here now in London
a young woman of 33 years
standing on a bridge carrying groceries
there I was a wild child
a little older than a toddler
fishing for fun with my grandfather,
under a weeping willow
on the rare hot summer evenings of Belarus
two canals, one water
perhaps it's true what they say

about home being everywhere
today I found a random piece of home
somewhere
where I was not looking for it
thank you

19.

thank you

20.

few things in life
bring more joy to my heart
and body
than eating butter
the house is in a state of chaos
the towels smell sufficiently begging me to clean
everyone's gone out to do
things and meet people
I am

eating butter on a british baguette

sitting on the afghan carpet sipping my already cold rosemary tea

in awe of the pottery I made

myself

surrounded by mess and dust

no pants

the silence

I'm eating butter

thank you

21.

visions keep us going

creating keeps my curiosity alive

always wondering

- what is next? -
- can I? -
- what if it works? -

as I took the time

today to think of my tomorrow

I came to bow to this girl

going
from relying on men to make her dreams come true
to becoming she who envisions and owns her future
thank you

22.

woke up confused about last night's crisis
- let it go
    not because you can't make it,
    not out of doubt for yourself
    but to learn to let go
    of anything that makes you doubt or grind
    let go
    of what you are most attached to
    and see yourself moving forward
    you may even find yourself flying
said the voice coming forth from a deep well inside of me
thank you

23.

and it's only by being still
that I can feel life move through and in me
I read a qi gong master said
the heart can live in the duality,
it can feel both sadness and happiness
in equal measure, whereas
the mind drowns in sorrow for the death of an elder
and forgets to rejoice the birth of a child
my heart cries on midsummer day
I sit down to write
searching like a hound
for feelings of gratitude
about the day that's been
I can find only sadness and new tears
I wish I could change the course of things
yet what do I know about those bigger plans
my heart cries
for my mom missing me and
her mom missing her, in three countries
our lineage scattered

one alone, one treated unkindly and one - me - treated
like neither of them could dream
I am their dream and their prayers answered
my heart cries for I cannot change their lives and encounters
from which I resulted
so I thank
I chose different for us all
who were and those who will come
may the next women of my lineage
know
worth, love, kindness
when stepping on Earth
thank you

24.

pleasure
laughter
food and
sex
all I can think of

on a night like this
tipsy on happiness and wine
sleeping next to a man
who enjoys as much as I do
life
thank you

25.

I finally took my education
seriously
as a citizen of this Earth
humanity always awaits
arms open
thank you
to learn wisdom from our grandparents
spontaneity from the children
and the rest from nature
those are the three teachers
I exiled myself from for so long
until today,
when the smile of a baby reminded me of the lightness

one feels after putting down the backpack at the end of a
full day of hike
thank you
my grandmother has survived war
and outlived her son's death
still she laughs and takes care of herself
thank you
for nature surrounds me, us
in infinite forms, speaking endless languages
up to each to grasp its message
thank you

26.

out of nowhere
surpassing me on my right
riding his bike
he cheered me up
- you're almost at the top!

thank you

27.

women
gathering
drinking wine
sharing feelings
thank you

28.

so much
I took for granted all my life
never really understood the old generations
who spent entire life times in one place
my grandfather's heart couldn't take it
the first time he left his home country
to visit his daughter
I would travel
without giving it too much thought
no destination really mattered
it was cheap
a convenient escape

not a trip
and now that I undustied my suitcase
I feel the baggage
of the journey I am to embark on
places have meaning again
destinations have purpose
time is precious
I am to become a traveller
thank you

29.

a home to come back to
like a rose's smell and
the last summer days
feels
thank you
I hardly recognise as mine the objects in my room
did I change this much?
have I grown up?
my parents are still the same
yet time touches them more profoundly every year

what a strange feeling to come back, maybe
I did not come back, maybe
I simply arrived
our encounter is infused with the present
for once I stand here as I am today
not as the daughter I was
even with my brother the slate is clear
so why do I cry?
because still I feel
thank you

30.

there are places where the mind switches off
go there
it's almost strange not to have plans nor deadlines
and you see the world still stands
it keeps on spinning
so I rest
thank you

31.

my brother
you teach me to love and accept
who thinks in opposite ways to mine
not every day I manage to look at you
with the eyes of my soul
however, I try
everytime I catch myself cursing at you
you speak of absolute truth
where I tell you pieces of truth reside in each heart
you speak of division
where I tell you I do not love all people yet I strive to believe in a people, humanity
you blame one for all that's wrong and unfair in this world
where I tell you there are no saints here and everyone has got their part
my brother
I feel that above our differences we are the same
see, we both care and we both want freedom for the people
it strikes me every time

to acknowledge how similar our hearts are
despite our intellects and views
is it the books we read? or the people we met? who influenced you?
I wished many times I could could go back
to a precise moment in time, maybe I could
change the course
maybe I could change you
what a selfish thought! - I know
so you teach me the hard way to love
pressing me on all my beliefs until I question my studies
and the world, because
why would I be right and you wrong?
I love you, my brother
after many years
I see us taking a step to meet
somewhere halfway
thank you

32.

the sound of the bells

the whispering of a gentle breeze
a turquoise sky and vivid green leaves
of hands that adjust
voices that speak
the popping of bottles
and of a pile of unread magazines
all that my return home feels
thank you

33.

cheers!
to a day that passed
swiftly
and I was not here to enjoy it
thank you

34.

it's funny how the forced quarantine

after a trip
forces my mind to reconnect to my body
at its own pace
physically I may be sitting on the hammock
in my home in London
whereas in reality I am sitting on Roda's back
going in circles
something about women and horses
what a gift this creature
and what a sense of relief to be carried
and feeling light
a woman on a horse can finally relax
someone stronger and with much wit
is there to take her to the end of the world
so I felt
something about women and horses
both forced to carry things and people
they'd rather not
often in silence, given a purpose
without first being asked about their own
it's only a horse, people say
it's just a woman, men say
yet at the end of a long summer day of work,

she still had the power to take from me
all my worrisome thoughts
thank you

35.

something wonderful happened
since I started buying plants
for the first time in my life
I was growing roots of my own
so today
I took care of my piece of eden
and removed dust from their leaves
a sense of happiness pervaded me
and I too felt compelled to come back
to my body
I have called home many places
and I am coming to find my one and only
where all the rest becomes
familiar places
of memories and lost hopes
my land with my green babies

is the eldorado
thank you

36.

thank you
for your understanding spirit
we balance well our impulsivities
thank you
for your guidance
even when I'm too stubborn to ask

37.

when we invited birds
on our balcony, we did not think
about the amount of cleaning
it would involve,
still when forced to decide
between absence of birds
and a sparkling balcony

we chose the family of seven sparrows
oh the life they bring along!
thank you

38.

walking on the canal
lost in an internal dialogue
I came to the conclusion
feelings live in details
not in a bunch of flowers
but in that one flower
not in grand promises
but in the one dinner prepared specially for me
not in a poetic jump into the unknown
but in a firm walking next to each other
thank you

39.

I never buy delicate plants
I do not care for flowers
I love more the green creatures, who
can thrive almost without me
yet I desired of welcoming an orchid
to my sacred garden
the most exquisite and delicate of all
you are
you are the crown
I wonder if I am worthy of such presence
you exude
please live with me
grant me your flowers
and whisper in my dreams your wish
welcome lady Orchid
thank you

40.

I have all
I have health
so how come do I need
to be reminded of it only by its absence
-     if wise enough
       it takes the absence in others
       to remind you of your own
thank you my body
thank you my spirit
thank you even to my mind
may I turn always to seek beauty

41.

I paid my car loan
a debt I had weighing on me
for two years, like a vulture over my shoulder
first I felt disoriented
like a slave whose chains are suddenly broke open
who am I without them?

where to go next?
I realise today how everything I did
was fuelled by the need
to pay off something and someone
sudden as lightning, a new opportunity came in
and I witnessed money flowing
in and out
smoothly
I'm debt-free
it must be an energy for I have not touched it
the path to freedom is exciting
beyond fear and uncertainty
I am starting to hear my heart
whisper its desires
thank you

42.

the other night
walkabouts with friends and Love
keep me company
today

thank you

43.

sometimes I wonder
what if the most beautiful flowers
are so beautiful because they are wishes
of those men and women who
passed away after having lived
the most righteous life possible
I wonder also if I could
be a good gardener for those souls
until the day far away
I will become a flower myself
if today there is one such soul
among the plants and flowers I take care of
I am honoured
thank you

44.

I had news of my babushka
it's very hot in Minsk, and she was bothered
by the state of the front porch of her building
so much trash and abandonment
                I cannot bare witness, she said
so she took her broom, and
spent two hours cleaning
happy and tired she returned home
thank you
the following day, weather was the same
she craved berries she could only get at the Kamarovka a
market the furthest from her home
no heat no pain in the leg no laziness could stop her
her desire burned stronger
happy and full she lied on the sofa
thank you
even from afar she gets to teach me lessons
at times I am so caught in another reality
I don't think about cleaning the streets I walk
instead I clean my feed
thank you

45.

my mother taught me freedom
since the day I was born
although I believed I had been abandoned
she fled, leaving me in the safest place,
to build a better future for us
cruel mother!
with that gesture she set the base
of my values in life
freedom
for myself
acceptance
for others
her choice that day, took me here today
neither her nor I could have survived long
in a dictatorship,
who knows what are the by-products of our choices?
especially when the choices we take are aligned with ourselves
I save lives as by-product
of my choice to get the vaccine only to be able to travel more freely

my mother did not sacrifice her happiness,
is that selfish?
or is that a valuable survival skill?
my mother taught me to be free
and harness my own happiness
thank you

46.

in the presence of certain women
words become unnecessary
eyes say it all
the mouth is enough to say *thank you*

47.

one glass was fine, I wanted it
the second was dictated by habit
yet a loving invisible presence
spilled it

it was bedtime for me, anyway
thank you

48.

I heard the voice of my babushka
she is well today
I feel sad I am not with her
but the news of a lady stranger who saved her life
fill my heart
may you live long!
one person is enough to reignite
my hope in humanity,
as long as there is one person left
not all is doomed
I may be far but there are people around her
thank you

49.

did you notice

when you do what you love
even if physically demanding, paired with little sleep
you recharge your energy
no draining occurs
that should be my compass
always
in addition the sun was shining
thank you

50.

I am filled with gratitude
for the women in my family
who taught me to cook
for I am now
earning a living with that skill
thank you

51.

turn toward the sun
I remind myself everyday
as old anger rises
maybe for the first time
I am finding the courage
to address it toward the right people
those I tried to protect, from
my resentment   my aching heart   my abandoned self
I feared so long casting a shadow upon those men, that
I am finding it uncomfortable to grow tall
and yet doesn't the birch tree grow
without ever feeling pity for the shrub?
after years of digging
I am able to finally see myself
I was not to be found in the ground, but by raising my eyes to the sky
thank you

52.

the rain so refreshing
cleansed me
once the cloudy thoughts were gone
a deep realisation rose
thank you

53.

today not only I showed up
but I came to rescue myself
after weeks of neglect,
I am so accustomed to survive
it's only when I'm one step from falling that I come take
my hand
I promised to never give up on myself
now I wonder
can I walk by my side everyday?
today I and I took the first step
and my loving partner knew to step aside
thank you

54.

a rarity
to find in this world of many self-proclaimed healers
one whose hands are truly guided,
by the elements and the angelic forces
what a treat to be massaged
my body surrendered, after years of craving said touch
with the sole purpose to be healed
thank you

55.

I asked intentionally
for a teacher,
she arrived
thank you

56.

onto an adventure Love and I
set
to visit sacred ancient grounds
I was reminded of the beauty
to physically see and live a place, even after
having seen it a thousand times depicted in a photograph
and yet in no photo could a raven fly to me to be fed strawberries from my hand
thank you

57.

what a marvellous sunday!
waking up naked
feeling free
early yoga in a private garden taught by my friend
and a long walk with Love
sipping coffee and indulging in philosophical talks
ending at home watching thunders and rain

from the window, whilst lying in bed
thank you

58.

the gentle breeze on my skin
that feeling of aliveness enveloping me
birds singing their farewell to the day
I am ecstatic
ah! the colourful food I cooked quenches my sight
how can simplicity be so good?
I take so much for granted
I can eat anything I desire, I'm safe
rocking on the hammock
this summer evening
thank you

59.

спасибо
merci

grazie
gacias
thank you
obrigada
danke
ありがとう
mulţumesc
dziękuję
faleminderit
I can thank
many faces I cross

60.

he left the guys
to come make me a burger
as promised
thank you
but oh, the rainbow
in front of me as I cycled
back home to him
thank you

61.

underneath this tired body
I feel utter joy
something I have never felt
at least not for this long
I must've nailed the equations
after year of trying
thank you

62.

why despair of a broken tyre
for it led to a cab ride
paid by the client
and a rest day for my legs
thank you

63.

the joy!

spending the morning shopping
for ingredients to cook new flavours
later cleaning my home
and spending time with my plants
I recharge to welcome guests tonight
thank you

64.

the power pleasure has
is unique
I am blessed to share it
with the man I love
so much sacredness is involved
in having sex
thank you

65.

I want to be healthy!
this thought did not leave me

in the past days
I've had teachers who taught me
the consequences of not taking care of myself
thank you
now I take care of my
body, through food and movement and pleasure
mind, through books and supplements and nature
spirit, through rituals and challenging old beliefs
everyday I bow to the holy trinity
within myself
knowing I can finally afford
the food, the supplements, the things
that increase my joy and mood
thank you

66.

I'm not sure what made me look up
from the grey concrete I was riding on
to the cloudy sky
but up there I saw possibility
coloured in baby blue

down here even puddles are grey
    - so look up! remember to look up
    from time to time! -
thank you
do you believe in past lives?
I received earthy gifts today
from a friend from afar
he reminds me of the joy
of parting from people, with love and peace
at the end of a lifetime
so we may meet again as friends
thank you

67.

today I got hit by Realisation
a Goddess as brutal as she is sweet
granting freedom to the soul that can withstand it
my grandmother woke up in a puddle of blood
once again saved by a good woman
Life must love her or
she is still among us only to keep on teaching me lessons

thank you - whatever the reason
in panic I search all the ways I can go visit her
simultaneously I begin the descent into the Goddess' realm
why now? suddenly you have the money to travel and the courage to lose your job
why not have gone while she was well and sane to enjoy walks together
instead you will be sitting at home, or at the hospital, watching the clock
did you want to go?
no
was she a priority then?
evidently not
maybe I don't want her to face the pain and fear alone,
for it is then that we take a closer look at who we are surrounded by
I feel guilty
I tried to blame the president of her country
it's him - his fault, he closed the borders
like all people in power, oblivious of the fact
families are scattered, they live across borders and seas
I feel anger

so I pick a fight with my partner
I feel everything only not to feel this pain, so deeply
that was the second wave of Realisation,
followed by a third: I am no better than a priest
I preach my father and mother and everyone to feel
yet I am scared of feeling honestly
can I survive the pains passing through my body on the way out of it?
today I sit with the Goddess of Realisation
I let her sink in
thank you

68.

I learned my first word in Korean
annyeong haseyo - hello
it's a start
thank you

69.

if my mind is confused
and goal driven
there's my body sending signals
and putting limits
thank you
honestly cheers to friday
and talks with my friend
thank you

70.

a road trip
with Friendship and Love as companions
to the seaside, Whitstable
on a very typical british summer day
we eat oysters with doughnuts
laughing soaking wet
what a welcome to this town
we laughed and laughed

until the sun came out to participate
thank you
a feast of seafood
unexpected finds
and gifts from nature
thank you
tired a little
we went on, to Canterbury and beyond
a short visit
of many more laughs, about little doors, of imaginary
carpenters with one leg short, and
a never found way to the Cathedral
all and nothing mattered the same
on this neverending day
thank you

71.

fresh flowers
and a date with myself
completed the day
thank you

72.

may all my loved ones
keep on being well and healthy and safe
thank you
I am so grateful
for the job that gives me the money I need
to buy all that I want
and go travel with my Love
thank you
a job that challenges my beliefs
and shows the inner work
I avoided to confront
thank you

73.

I am thankful for the life
I paved for myself
I am thankful for the flowers
I hold in my hand
I am blessed by the rays of light

the sun is touching my skin
thank you
thank you
thank you
I bless each and every one
of those sharing Mother Earth with me

74.

it took
32 years of my life
20 years of work
0 money put aside
to finally step in and take myself along with my future
into my own hands
today is the day
I've felt the most powerful, ever
thank you

75.

bullet points of gratitude:
- being appreciated at work
- selling clothes I don't wear anymore
- meeting my friend
- passing the evening talking, soul digging and walking
- not drinking alcohol, as would be my usual

thank you

76.

Love came back
and immediately found its home
between my legs
infusing my temple with joy
desire and pleasure
thank you

77.

I was reading
about the impermanence of life
when I noticed the river flowing
somehow I find comfort
in being a drop
nothing and everything, for I shall
never forget I contain the ocean in me
thank you

78.

my period came just on time
to finish before we leave for Portugal
thank you
today I am pervaded with a sense
of accomplishment
the kind, a procrastinator only can feel
bravo! to me
this time
when I say I do

it's different
thank you

79.

to sometimes forgetting time
and all the shoulds
thank you

80.

my strong body
begging me to stop
    - take a break, I'm tired!!
soon ... one more day
keep it strong, you are
I nurture you well
and I will find a way
to take care of you
the way we take care of others
one more day
thank you

81.

a day recollecting lessons
my job teaches me
I agreed to keep working
even if it doesn't inspire me
and it changes my mood and I always wish
I was doing something else
I count the minutes
8 hours feel eternal
   - how can people spend 50 years in a job like that? -
I know I do it for money
and here it is the story of our world today
I chose to be in this
for 1 year and the lessons are many
the most important being: this is the last time
thank you

82.

I stood in the middle of the room
surrounded by the concrete

immersed in the grey colour, I thought
some people are poor and stay poor
no matter the amount of money
this thought broke through the erroneous vision
I had of myself
because in that moment I felt rich
rich in passions
rich in colours
rich in talents
rich in resources
rich in possibilities
all reflected in my tiny home
whereas they had money and nothing else
I am rich in love
I am rich in taste
I am rich in beauty
I am rich in plants
I am rich
thank you

82.

day off!
thank you

83.

this morning we landed in Lisbon
the palms so vivid in contrast to the pale sky
I search for the horizon
the smell of salty water
cleanses my soul
as my eyes can't get enough of
soaking in the beauty
after a full day
in a city I have never been to
feasting on fish and mussels
Love and I sat on the couch
gazing at the full moon rising
above the sea
thank you

84.

where to begin to say many thanks?
how does a day of no plans turn into missed wishes
and a fight in the street can actually be a look into old wounds and shattered air castles
oh this full moon!
so much fire in Love and I fueled by this southern sky
which stayed impressed on my face
thank you so much
we grew closer and deeper
I realised I have my father's traits
the very same I judge
that his father gifted him
our subconscious played out, we got hurt
then acknowledged our wrongs
and seeked forgiveness from each other
thank you
at the end of the day
the sea, its waves
our sorrows takes
thank you

85.

thank you
the alarm rang before nature's waking hour
he prepared coffee
and we set on an adventure
an unusual foggy morning set the tone
in this wild land - chosen haven of our vacation
we drive getting lost a few times
and park confused unable to see much ahead of our nose
there's no connection to check if we're right
yet we are right
caught by surprise by the mediterranean aromatherapy
we descent, our senses heightened
our bodies touched by all the shrubs,
we don't know where we're going, then
the view opens, shy and pale
behind the fog's vale
we find ourselves above our desired destination, and
I can't but wonder whether what we desired was better than the path chance took us on
we're almost at the car when I stop, called by an Aleppus

pine
I drink its dew, lick its needles, smell it, shower under it
its dew is in my hair and I'm laughing like a child
I feel euphoric! I am the tree!
I collect wild fennel
I breath in wild rosemary
I still have my wild
thank you

86.

I spent the better part of the day   reading
later, nearly at sunset
when the sun actually made its first appearance today
we went to a place that felt like home
there I bathed and swam
in the fresh waters of the ocean
and found a small cave looking like a vagina
secreting clay to cleanse ones body
no token to pay
a display of the Mother's abundance
everyone could take, she has so much to give

enough for my body and yours and theirs
I took
and laughed and thanked
thank you
thank you
thank you

87.

pleasure is on the other side of the cold
pleasure is on the other side of the cold
I repeated this mantra, as I made my way into the ocean
children don't seem concerned with the low temperature of the water
they aren't anticipative of the cold enveloping their tiny bodies,
they just jump straight into the ocean, high on laughter
I noticed this time the cold is also less severe for me
can it be that I stopped being afraid of it?
a wave hits me, impatient to get me fully wet
I surrender in laughter, there is nothing else
I'm a child again

and so I say yes to play,
the wave comes back intent on getting my swimsuit off
I dive in and under
I let my body roll
I resurface to take a breathe
I laugh
it's sunset, the wind is gentle
I'm just a child playing with the ocean
thank you

88.

we drove through a natural reserve
I witnessed the magnificence of a snake plant
when not contained in a vase
which makes me think of the birds kept in cages, or any animal kept in a zoo for the matter
forced to sing for their master rather than the world
losing just a little of its beauty and life
I contemplated a semi wild beauty while laying on a surfer's beach
and collected rocks - my favourite pastime

ending this last day drinking prosecco on a rooftop with some artist friends
and stumbling at a book fair - another one of my favourite pastimes
I rejoiced being surrounded by foreign words
I still felt we were all speaking the same language, of those who love stories and words
thank you

89.

the road home
between the clouds
is clear
thank you

90.

I am thankful
for I have seen and touched
the life of my dreams

and will make it happen
where dreams and life collide
creating magic and abundance
thank you

91.

I entered the field
of someone truthful
whose power stems from the heart
I will forever be changed
thank you
tonight I tasted my own power
and I was not scared
as it did not stem from ego
thank you

92.

one object I am absolutely thankful for
the immersion blender I bought

will most certainly make my winter warmer and healthier
thank you
one intangible thing I am thankful for
the courses I enrolled in
thank you
one person I am thankful for
my mother
both sunshine and cloud, on alternate days
thank you

93.

this morning, while drinking coffee
I secretly desired cookies
later, when I got home from work
I was welcomed by a gift:
he got me my favourite cookies
thank you

94.

flowers
there's a gorgeous yellow flower
in the garden where I work
it stands and radiates all its beauty
regardless of my eye on it
it teaches me to receive
thank you

95.

still I show up
in front of this paper
thank you
to experience a full day
a walk, a coffee and pain au chocolat
having money to buy good meat
and brunching
thank you

96.

while tidying up
and sorting my books
will I read this at last, or will I not?
I came across a book I found
on the street at 6am on my way to work
many months ago
I have forgotten about it
and now I'm all in, like
satiated after hunger
thank you

97.

how can one be happy after 13 hours of work?
yet I am
I'm flying with excitement
as we're supposed to feel
tired and energised
thank you

98.

some books are meant to be written, others read
I often find parts and pieces of myself
in pages written by others
isn't this wonderful?
I am not alone
and when I doubt I can survive
a story proves me wrong
thank you

99.

I called upon my ancestors
they met me in a space
inside of me
where I dissolves into we
thank you

100.

little beer
little aperol spritz
guys chat
business inevitably
I got advice
my personal green card to start
thank you
and so I notice
100 days of commitment
I awe it to myself to say
thank you

101.

Love and I
went to the cinema
we went to the cinema after two years
of watching movies naked in bed
artists of time, sometimes a movie could last days
I was not used to sitting still for so long

taking it all in one go
but oh did I enjoy the popcorn, sweet and salty for me
then on the short walk to our home
we discussed what we just saw
sharing our favourite scenes
an intellectual game I missed, which enables thoughts to sediment
at home we'd turn off the light and say goodnight
what a great invention the cinema
thank you

102.

of all the things I receive for free
sunshine on a sunday morning in September
with coffee on the terrace
overlooking the canal
it's my favourite thing
thank you
thank you
thank you
so much

103.

again the urge to do
I have an imaginary schedule
to follow
I have to tick boxes
people expect - do they?
so I took a nap
allowed myself to take a bath
and in that moment of nothingness, came to me
the ending of a novella I wrote over 3 years ago
and so rebelling against my imaginary plans
I wrote immersed for hours
thank you

104.

a child gifted me a thank you sticker
with a rainbow
another child flooded me with smiles
I felt so rich inside
children are a good influence

they are born rich, pure, enlightened
who knows
I may one day become enlightened playing with them
rather than reading books on spirituality
they make me feel special when they choose me
thank you

105.

today I was reminded
of how sweet friendship is
and how empty a life
without meaningful connections is
I remind myself that friendship has many faces
and it changes them with time, in a game
I came to love the face of friendship today in my life
thank you

106.

it's Love
Love will save us all
no therapy can compare
the love of a partner who comes to the rescue when the
other is blocked and triggered
today, by dropping everything - even work
to come lie with me
in the anguish of my silence
you Love, broke down barriers
with your mere presence and the strongest hug
how many more lessons will you teach me?
thank you

107.

I discovered my voice thanks to a baby
I sang her mantras
until she felt safe to fall asleep
I remember that as a child I used to sing
not to make it a profession

but for a pure delight of the senses
I sing today
thank you

108.

I am born for more
than just cleaning someone else's ass
than doing someone else's laundry
than feeding someone else's children
and yet I passed through those doors
to learn that exists in this world
to learn about being underappreciated
and underpaid
and not seen
and not heard
part of an army of hidden slaves
until I lit a candle in my heart
then brought it to the attic to illuminate all the dark corners
I found so much dust, old clothes, cobwebs, dirt, old photographs, diaries of rules and beliefs

I set it on fire
may you turn to ashes
I use to fertilise my soil, for new seeds
thank you

Thank You

With these poems I have probably acknowledged everyone and everything for a lifetime, nonetheless I'd like to make a few specific names.
I want to thank first and foremost my darling partner Alex, who has been through it all and inspired me to change the way I approach work. Thank you for your creativity and patience in helping me birth this book, and for pushing me to believe in myself.
In 2021 I was also lucky enough to be surrounded by successful women who inspired me to become more of myself. Thank you dear Estelle for our long walks on the weekends, in Hackney. Our endless chats about life, magic, books, dreams, have been and continue to be a great source of well being and strength.
I also want to thank all the children that I've been guided to look after: you have been my greatest teachers and transformed my life. There are obviously so many more people I am grateful to have in my life that contributed indirectly to this book. My family who I love dearly, my babushka. My new French family, you always make me feel at home, thank you.
I like to thank life for making everything possible. Lastly, I thank myself for always creating, always writing, always going forward, always gathering lessons and always evolving.

About the author

Tanya is a writer of multiple genres, from poetry, to fairytales, to children's books, to memoires - both in Italian and in English.

She is an indie author and poétesse of Belarusian, Italian and German heritage, living in London.
She published in Italy with Europa Edizioni her first book, Della Bellezza e Del Silenzio - a poetry collection that captures those moments of rupture in the soul, transforming them into the beauty of experience.
She is the founder of IN HER GENIUS, a website collecting stories of women who live their life as an expression of their essence, so as to leave a testimony and trace of an often ignored extraordinary existence.

She lives fully, feels deeply and loves sweetly.

Printed in Poland
by Amazon Fulfillment
Poland Sp. z o.o., Wrocław